THE
CONTENT
BEAST

THE CONTENT BEAST

CREATE STORY-DRIVEN CONTENT TO CONNECT WITH YOUR AUDIENCE

GEOFFREY KLEIN

GRIFFON KEELEY PRESS

Praise for *THE CONTENT BEAST*

"I love how approachable this book is. *The Content Beast* demystifies the creation and distribution of content, and makes it viable for all businesses and individuals. Bravo!"
JAY BAER, New York Times best-selling author of *Youtility: Why Smart Marketing is About Help not Hype*

"Modern business owners face a unique challenge in capturing their audience's attention. *The Content Beast* by Geoffrey Klein provides a guide to creating and sharing compelling content that cuts through the noise and captivates your target market. This book is a must-read for entrepreneurs, marketers, and anyone seeking to improve their content marketing efforts."
MELINDA EMERSON, SmallBizLady, Best-selling author, *Become Your Own Boss in 12 Months*

"*The Content Beast* is a terrific collection of content marketing wisdom, stories, and tools that you will use every day. Geoffrey lays out what you need to think, do, and say to emotionally connect in today's hyper-noisy environment. If you want to win more attention, build stronger relationships, and sell your ideas and services - more easily and more often - follow every single step that Geoffrey lays out in this masterful book. Buy a copy for everyone on your team. Yes, it's that good!"
DAVID NEWMAN, Best-selling author of *Do It! Marketing* and *Do It! Selling*

"In a world that insists you create more content, it's worth knowing the why, the what, and the how? Geoffrey Klein is the king of content creation, and with *The Content Beast* in your corner you'll quickly learn how to create killer content that connects with your audience."
MICHAEL HEPPELL, Sunday Times #1 Best-selling author, Speaker and Coach

"A fun and useful approach to content marketing. Geoffrey Klein's *The Content Beast* will teach you how to craft narratives that resonate deeply with your audience, using techniques rooted in the science of story. With an engaging, conversational style, *The Content Beast* is an easy read that provides straightforward and practical steps to level up your content marketing game."
ADAM MARKEL, co-founder of WorkWell and Wall Street Journal best-selling author of *Change Proof: Leveraging the Power of Uncertainty to Build Long-Term Resilience*

"Got a business? Need to create content? *The Content Beast* should be your North Star! Geoffrey Klein is a pro and lays it all out for you, everything you need to know to feed the beast delicious content. Read it. Do it.
LU ANN CAHN, eight-time Emmy award-winning investigative journalist and author of *I Dare Me*

"The content marketing world can be overwhelming, but *The Content Beast* breaks it down into manageable pieces. Discover the science behind captivating narratives and how to implement them into your content marketing. Whether you're a seasoned marketer or just starting out,

Geoffrey equips you with the tools and techniques to elevate your content strategy and create a meaningful connection with your audience."
RAMON RAY, author of *Celebrity CEO,* motivational speaker and event host and a leading expert on personal branding and small business growth

The Content Beast is a friendly, creative, and straightforward look at content marketing, a topic that many people still don't seem to grasp but will soon need given the upcoming changes to the marketing landscape. I especially liked Geoffrey's concept of "infobesity," a creative take on the term "information overload," encapsulating the idea that we're all so inundated with information that we're all about to explode. The only way to compete is to systematically approach both targeting and content creation to get through the noise and "feed the beast" with the right content at the right time. Luckily, Geoffrey does just that in the later chapters of the book. If you're looking for a fast, friendly approach to both learning and executing a content strategy, check this book out!
MARK DE GRASSE, President of DigitalMarketer.com and author of *The Future of Content Marketing*

GRIFFON
KEELEY
PRESS

DEDICATION

For my favorite audience - my family

Nita
Jemma, Lucy, and Ethan

Table of Contents

Part 4
HOW TO FEED THE CONTENT BEAST............**61**

NOTE: You will find worksheets, bonuses, and companion tools that can be downloaded, printed, and shared with your team by visiting thecontentbeast.co.

Creativity is intelligence having fun.
- Albert Einstein

Imagine this...

Your Kingdom

Every business, whether they know it or not, has a hungry beast waiting to be fed.

Imagine your business is a kingdom full of your products or services waiting inside your castle walls to serve your loyal subjects.

Unfortunately, the only entrance to the castle is the iron gate at the front – and it is there that the Content Beast lives. When hungry, the Content Beast is red and angry, its sharp teeth bared, showcasing hostility and readiness to fight.

In this state, the Content Beast is indeed very scary to anyone who approaches the castle. In fact, word of the status of the Content Beast is spread quickly to everyone far and wide.

If the Content Beast is not fed, everyone stays away from the castle.

On the flip side, when the Content Beast is well fed, it turns a calming purple.

In this satisfied state, it begins to sing its beautiful song. The satiated Content Beast's song is enchanting and inviting and carries its melodious sound far and wide to those loyal subjects in search of the products and services your castle provides.

Like a pied piper, the tune of the beast attracts everyone to the castle to explore your wares and, more often than not, buy what you are selling.

As such, every business needs to feed the Content Beast in order to transform him from a grumpy, scary creature that keeps customers or clients away to a gentle, welcoming creature that attracts the audience you seek to serve.

Traditionally, when we think of a beast, we imagine mythical creatures. Generally, the notion is a negative concept.

When it comes to content marketing, this is not necessarily the case. There is a meaning of a beast that is positive. It describes someone extremely talented.

You may hear people describe a sports figure as being a beast on the field or a professional being a beast at their job.

Ironically, the goal of this book is to turn you into a Content Feeding Beast – someone who masters the art and science of connecting to your customers to advance your business in a powerful and significant manner.

The Content Beast Three Ways

This book's title has three meanings. The Content Beast - the creature that needs to be fed is the primary meaning of the title.

It also signifies the business person who becomes a Content Beast – meaning someone who understands content and can produce a lot of valuable and relevant content.

Finally, it can be read slightly differently when the word content is used as an adjective to describe the beast being in a state of happiness. In this version, the beast is contented.

You can think of it like this – You need to feed the Content Beast by becoming a Content Beast yourself, and when you do, you turn the Content Beast (the hungry, agitated creature) into the Content Beast (satisfied).

PART 1

WHY
YOU NEED TO FEED
THE CONTENT BEAST

Information overload occurs when
the amount of input to a system
exceeds its processing capacity.
- Bertram Gross

We are drowning in information,
while starving for wisdom.
- E.O. Wilson

In these modern times, creating and sharing compelling content is more important than ever. There is an unfortunate truth that is impacting all businesses equally – the struggle of our audience. The clients or customers that we are working so hard to connect with are all suffering from not one but two pandemics: Infobesity and Short Attention Spans.

Infobesity

During stressful times, many people may be coping by overindulging in food and drink. Obesity is a major problem across the world that continues to persist and cause challenges for many. Unfortunately, there is yet another type of pandemic afflicting all of us –

INFOBESITY. Also known as information overload.

The term *information overload* is credited to Bertram Gross, a professor of political science at Hunter College, in his 1964 work – *The Managing of Organizations*.

It was later popularized in 1970 by Alvin Toffler, the American writer and futurist, in his book *Future Shock*.

Gross defined information overload as follows:

"Information overload occurs when the amount of input to a system exceeds its processing capacity."

Infobesity is a creative blend based on the words *information* and *obesity* (the condition of being overweight in a way which is unhealthy).

While the concept has existed in different forms for a long time, the advent of digital technology and the acceleration of data creation and distribution platforms from which to consume it have compounded the problem.

Due to the rise of the share culture, 24-7 access to internet/email/social media, and now the incredible moment-to-moment real-time feeds of mobile devices with infinite scrolls, there is indeed an overload of information – both being created and consumed.

Big Data has gotten bigger and faster. According to IBM Marketing Cloud:

Every day, we create 2.5 quintillion bytes of data. To put that into perspective, 90 percent of the data in the world today has been created in the last two years alone – and with new devices, sensors and technologies emerging, the data growth rate will likely accelerate even more.

Consider what happens every sixty seconds online.

From 2016 to 2021, AllAccess.com and Lori Lewis published the amazing infographic This Is What Happens In An Internet Minute. Then, for whatever reason, in 2022 it didn't appear. Thankfully, in 2023, eDiscovery Today and LTMG took up the mantle to produce the 2023 version of the infographic.

Here are a few highlights:

- 2.4 million Google searches
- Over 240 million emails are sent
- Over 10 million viewing minutes on Instagram
- Almost 7 million emojis sent
- Over 22,000 visits to ChatGPT

[**NOTE:** For a copy of the PDF and other companion tools go to thecontentbeast.co]

Just think about when you wake in the morning and check your email/phone and see a glut of new information – some important, much not.

The information superhighway is accessible every day, every hour, every minute. As more and more information is produced, how are we coping?

Information overload is clearly affecting our mental states as we worry about FOMO (Fear Of Missing Out).

How are brands changing the way they communicate in response to infobesity?

How is this reality impacting our thoughts on content marketing?

Over the last few decades, the marketing paradigm has shifted from marketers passively pushing out content to the masses to one in which one-to-one engagement is crucial.

Information, content creation, and distribution are more important than ever.

The result has been the proliferation of a myriad of platforms, tools, and even entire companies that aim to help businesses and brands create, curate, and share data.

Content marketing has arisen as a powerful and entirely independent discipline. While there is a push to find ways to make sense of big data, what do we do with all that little data – the constant stream of information that bombards us every waking moment and waits for us while we sleep?

We are a culture not only obsessed with our mobile devices but also the stream of content they deliver.

We never want to fall behind on the latest and greatest (or not so great) news and trends, but it is impossible to stay on top of it, let alone all the other data being produced.

ICYMI (In Case You Missed It)) has even arisen as an attempt to catch up on information you may not even have seen.

It is a vicious cycle, and there is no way to get up to speed, as the pace of information is much faster than its consumption.

As we look for ways to mine through the overabundance of information being "shared" with us, brands would do well to consider the audience's predicament of information overload.

Among all the noise created by so much volume, how can brands seeking to engage and reach customers or potential customers be heard?

Frequently, the result is that the Content Beast - while constantly looking to be fed a steady diet of relevant, valuable content – is confused and overwhelmed by the immense glut of content, which may lead to a state of paralysis.

Or the Content Beast gorges on the buffet of extraneous and irrelevant junk food of information that is unsatisfying and ends up with a content bellyache.

The Content Beast often has tremendous difficulty distinguishing between content that is unhealthy and content that is worthy of its attention.

Short Attention Spans

Speaking of attention – the ability to capture the attention of its audience is vital for any business to win at content marketing.

If a company cannot grab someone's attention, it has lost before it has even begun.

Even if you create amazing, relevant, valuable content - if you cannot get someone's attention – it is all for naught.

More bad news on this front – as human beings we continue to have shorter and shorter attentions spans.

I don't have a short attention…

Ooh, look a kitten!

It's that easy. With the constant barrage of information hurtling at us, is it any wonder that we cannot concentrate and that we are easily distracted?

With the rise of modern technology is the decline of human attention spans.

According to research, in 2000, a study was done to measure the average human attention span. It was 12 seconds (that in itself is pretty low).

The attention span of a goldfish is 9 seconds.

Today, the average human attention span is 8 seconds.

Yes, that's right folks, our attention span is less than that of a goldfish.

As such, I thank you for giving me your attention as I try to help you capture what matters most to your business.

Goldfish Myth

The story about the human attention span being less than a goldfish's appears to be a bit fishy (pun intended).

It may be that while this story is often cited and shared, this in itself does not make it valid or accurate.

More than a few have debunked the attention span goldfish myth.

When I first came across this story, I was immediately intrigued – it was good content. It helped support my idea of the power of story as a catalyst to grabbing people's attention.

The origin that is often cited of the human-goldfish attention gap came from a very reliable source: Microsoft.

When you look even a bit deeper, however, it appears that the study Microsoft conducted references the attention-gap from another source:

The Statistic Brain, which has been determined not to provide any real evidence for the claim.

This did not stop authoritative sources from *The New York Times, USA Today, Time* magazine, or *The Telegraph* from reporting that very catchy headline about diminishing attention spans.

I share the above for two important reasons.

One, I want to be transparent and not simply share "facts" that seem to support my overall thesis.

Two, is to warn you to take all "authoritative" information with a healthy pinch of salt.

While the human-goldfish comparison may not be reliable, the need to feed the Content Beast attention-grabbing content that contains value remains true.

You need to communicate that your content matters and prove it is worth paying attention to. It's less about length and more about relevance.

Attention is still the most precious resource in engagement.

Without being able to capture someone's attention, you have no shot at engaging with them.

It is the audience that does, in fact, *give* you their attention.

It is not so much that you can **take** someone's attention - but rather you must present content to attract the audience in order for them to **give** you their attention.

The primary objective when feeding the Content Beast is to garner enough attention and provide enough value that the audience connects with your message and then takes action — the action you want them to take to be closer to engaging with your product or service. Easier said than done.

I myself, like many others, suffer from shiny object syndrome. There is always something new and shiny to pull our focus from one thing to another that promises something more interesting and worthy of our attention.

The attention span issue relates back to the problem of infobesity. There is simply more content vying for our attention.

Our attention is like a pinball as we are shot out into a world of overwhelming sensory overload with targets of lights and sounds, often out of control, as we desperately try to keep ourselves in the game.

In our attempts to stay alive and rack up points, we never have enough time or wherewithal to gain any meaningful interaction, so in the end we fall down between our flippers without satisfaction or fulfillment.

Understanding the challenge of capturing attention spans is critical to having a successful business that connects with its potential and current customers.

What Is Your Biggest Challenge With Creating Content?

- Not enough time
- Not enough money
- Not enough ideas
- Lack of organization
- Lack of creativity
- Maintaining consistency
- Quality content
- Volume of content
- Providing value
- Establishing relevancy

Top of Mind

The combination of infobesity and the need to capture attention spans is a powerful one-two punch in our desire to share our message with our audience. The speed at which information is shared and the speed at which our attention is distracted by such information necessitates a steady flow of your content to keep in front of your audience.

Feeding the Content Beast, in the first instance, is about ensuring that your audience is aware of you. The current marketing landscape also requires you to continually feed more information more often to stand out from the content of your competitors and the content of other attention-sucking content.

Often, people reference the marketing rule of 7's that states that a potential customer must see a message at least 7 times before they'll be provoked to take an action.

As the amount of content increases and the number of ways to reach people expands, it becomes even more necessary to meet the demand and simply remind your audience you exist – let alone provide the relevant and valuable content that will motivate them to engage.

Why Not Give Up?

The concept of feeding the Content Beast may be as overwhelming as the concept of infobesity. With these incredible challenges and obstacles, the idea of connecting in a meaningful way to our audience seems extremely daunting.

The Content Beast is not a monster. Most of us are either willfully or blindly unaware of its existence – as we prefer to bury our heads in the sand rather than consider what appears to be an unsurmountable task.

This is understandable, though ignoring a problem will not make it go away.

Of course, like any problem, the first step is to admit you have one.

Once we recognize that feeding the Content Beast is not optional but necessary, then we can turn our attention to learning different techniques and approaches to tackle the issue.

While the primary problem is to find out how to feed the Content Beast, it is important to understand the overarching desire to connect with our audience. It is from this vantage point that I invite you to read on.

We continue this journey by asking a few more questions which are critical to unlocking the power to feed the Content Beast.

PART 2

WHO
ARE YOU REALLY FEEDING?

To have great poets, there must be great audiences.
- Walt Whitman

While the goal of this book is to share the importance of feeding the Content Beast, it is not the Content Beast you are ultimately looking to satisfy.

The real target of your content is your prospective or current customer.

When we talk about creating valuable and relevant content – Valuable to whom? Relevant to whom?

Your audience – the ones that will buy from you.

This may seem obvious, though many businesses both big and small generate lots of content that does not necessarily take into consideration the perspective of the right audience.

As mentioned earlier, relying on producing lots of content is a shortsighted strategy *IF* that content doesn't connect with the audience you are trying to reach.

While we will dive into the What and How to feed the Content Beast in later sections, we need to begin the process by asking WHO this content is for.

11ᵀᴴ Commandment

By gaining an understanding of who your audience is, you will have a much better chance of determining what kind of content to create and how to reach that audience.

If you remember nothing else from this book, remember the 11th Commandment:

KNOW THY AUDIENCE.

It is the foundational principle for good content marketing (and marketing in general). If you don't know your audience, good luck trying to connect with them. While people sometimes talk about a great salesperson who could sell snow to the Eskimos – wouldn't it be much easier to sell snow to people who live in a desert?

Knowing your audience is critical because then you can identify what they need, what they want, what they care about.

Learning what makes a potential customer tick is akin to having the key to the gate of opportunity.

The old adage that knowledge is power is certainly true in this case, and the more knowledge you have of those you are trying to connect with, the better you'll be able to do so.

Nobody Cares About What You Can Do

Too much content is created to showcase the incredible features (and benefits) of an organization. "We're the best," "Award-winning team," "We've been in business for over 80 years," "We're number 1," "Ranked numero uno!" The harsh but important reality is that nobody cares about how long you've been in business or how many awards you have received. Nobody cares about what you can do.

I find when I share this with business professionals, they are not too happy about it.

"What do you mean nobody cares about what we can do?"

It's true. People only care about what you can do...**for them!**

You have to realize that every consumer listens to the same radio station all the time - - the most popular radio station of all – WII-FM.

Which stands for: *What's In It For Me?!*

Even if you have the best product or service, if it doesn't help their situation, they don't care. A brand can truly have game-changing technology or innovative process, but if it fails to address the need - - the pain of your audience – it is a failure.

Focus on the customer. This is another simple yet often ignored business approach. You may think you are attracting people by puffing up your chest and standing tall with a parade of accolades – no one cares.

Consumers are looking to connect with brands that deliver on their needs and solve their problems. They also want brands to align with their values, their interests, and their feelings.

It is not only worth the time, but it also has become essential to understand and to genuinely care about your customer.

25

Nobody cares how much you know,
until they know how much you care.
-Theodore Roosevelt

Stop Selling And Start Caring

The way to show your customers you care is by knowing them – the more you know, the better you can create powerful content to illustrate your interest in them.

Also, when you know a lot about your customers, it becomes much easier to identify them and target them with relevant, valuable content.

The other problem I often encounter with businesses looking to feed the Content Beast is that they think everyone is their customer.

When I ask who is their ideal customer, they reply with "anyone" or "everyone."

My response to that notion is to wish them well in trying to market to that broad audience.

This harkens back to the old traditional paradigm where a single marketing message was broadcast to a large, wide audience. This strategy has two big problems.

First, you likely will waste resources by sharing a message with people who have no interest or intention of ever engaging, let alone purchasing, your product or service.

Second, the message will be so general that it won't resonate deeply enough, even with those that would be inclined to pay attention and consider the content further.

One of the great benefits of digital marketing is its ability to target specific audiences. Once you know your audience well, it then becomes much easier to target them and to tailor your content so it connects with them.

The more relevant your content is to your audience, the more they will respond to it. My friend Bob Bentz summed it up well in his book *Relevance Raises Response.*

While Bob's book was geared to the mobile marketing audience, its concept of developing and sharing relevant content to a specific audience is powerful and important to maximizing your content marketing efforts.

Your audience is one single reader. I
have found that sometimes it helps
to pick out one person-a real person
you know, or an imagined person-
and write to that one.
- John Steinbeck

Get To Know Them

The advent of digital marketing has enabled brands to get to know their customers better than ever.

Traditional media relied on broad, general knowledge of a given population and had to extrapolate a lot of missing pieces.

It was and continues to be difficult to gather reliable data on a wide group of a particular audience without great effort and expense. Even so, the results are rarely as accurate or insightful as you would like.

The digital landscape is able to fill in the gaps in incredibly efficient and effective ways to gather intel on any given group. Digital advertising is built upon the foundational ability to target or segment the audience you are trying to reach.

A study conducted by the University of Cambridge and Stanford University showed that Facebook knows you better than your friends do.

As time has gone on, the platforms we use online are more and more sophisticated at capturing and tracking our behavior (and some would argue influencing our decisions/actions) to an alarming degree, which enables marketers to target very specifically those people that they believe will be best suited to offer their product or service to.

Powerful Tool That's Always Available

We all possess a very powerful tool for learning about our audience. We have this tool with us all the time- every day, every minute, every second.

No – not our phones (though sadly the above may be true).

This powerful tool is what bookends our brains – **our ears.** Use the power of listening to find out what matters to your audience. Listening leads to learning.

Demographics vs. Psychographics

There are two big buckets of characteristics that we can and should gather about our target audience. The first bucket is known as demographics, and the second bucket is known as psychographics.

Demographics are generally things that are certain and known. Where does someone live? What age are they? What income bracket do they fall into? Here is a general list of demographics you should know about your target audience:

- Age
- Gender
- Sexual orientation
- Ethnicity
- Geography
- Residential status
- Education level completed

- Relationship status
- Family status
- Disabilities
- Income
- Profession

Demographics identify groups based on information about their identity and are typically easier to identify and understand.

The other bucket, psychographic data, is about how people think and feel. Often underrated, psychographics can be exceptionally valuable.

These characteristics of your audience include their interests, activities, and opinions. Here is a list of some of the traits that would be helpful to know:

- Personality
- Values
- Attitudes
- Beliefs
- Interests and activities
- Lifestyles
- Media consumption

Psychographic characteristics can greatly enhance your ability to create content to feed the Content Beast. At first glance, the list may seem broad and general.

Once you start to gather data on a customer, it becomes much clearer how these tools can be helpful. Psychographics could include sports that someone either follows or plays.

It could be their interest in political or social causes. Information about what they believe in and their behavior will lead to an understanding of *how* they make purchasing decisions.

By knowing their beliefs, what they care about and what they do not care about, you can align your marketing messages more closely to their beliefs and increase your connection to the very people you want to connect with.

When it comes to knowing your audience, it is not a matter of choosing one bucket over the other. It is when you combine the information that you can start to create a fuller picture.

If you do not use these opportunities to understand your customer, then all the effort you make to create content to feed the Content Beast is really just guesswork, and potentially a waste of time and energy.

Buyer Persona

Understanding your audience is critical, though sometimes simply having a long list of characteristics may leave you feeling a bit overwhelmed. Thankfully, there is a tool that marketers use to aggregate the data into a helpful snapshot of your ideal audience: the Buyer Persona (or Avatar).

A buyer persona is a fictional representation of an ideal customer. It is used to help businesses better understand the needs, behaviors, and preferences of their target market.

Buyer personas are typically developed through a combination of market research, interviews, and surveys. They are used to inform marketing campaigns and product development decisions.

Buyer personas are important in content marketing because they provide content creators with a better understanding of their target audience.

Knowing who your target audience is and what they want to hear will inform the type of content you create and how it is presented.

This helps ensure that your content resonates with your audience and drives conversions.

Here are 5 benefits to creating a Buyer Persona:

1. **Improved targeting**
    Buyer personas help you identify the right people to target with your content. You will be able to create content that is more relevant to your audience and increase the likelihood of conversion.

2. **Increased engagement**
    By understanding your buyer personas, you will be able to create content that resonates with them, driving more engagement and better results.

3. **Better ROI**
    By targeting the right people with content that resonates, you will be able to generate more qualified leads and better ROI.

4. **Improved alignment**
    Buyer personas help align all marketing efforts to meet the needs and interests of the target audience.

5. **More effective content**
    With the help of buyer personas, you will be able to create content to feed the Content Beast that is more effective in engaging and converting customers.

By creating a detailed buyer persona, businesses can better understand the motivations and preferences of potential customers and customize their products, services, and marketing strategies to meet their needs.

Fictional buyer personas also help businesses to identify areas where they could improve their offerings and better serve their customers.

For our purposes, this fictional character will inform the type of content to create, as well as how to communicate it in the most effective way to connect with your audience.

Different marketers will have slightly different Buyer Personas though most of the relevant elements should be present.

These include:

- Name
- Age

- Location
- Occupation
- Income
- Family
- Goals/Motivations
- Buying behaviors
- Pain points
- Communication preferences

You'll notice these resemble the same demographic and psychographic information we discussed earlier. This is not an accident.

Creating the Buyer Persona profile is about synthesizing the data of your customers or potential customers to create that snapshot of your ideal target audience.

Let's take a look at an example to illustrate what a Buyer Persona should look like.

Imagine you own a car dealership, and you have a good deal of data on what you believe your ideal customer looks like.

Creating a Buyer Persona can confirm and clarify your sense of that persona.

Name: Jane Doe
Age: 28
Location: Seattle, WA
Occupation: Software Engineer
Income: $110,000
Family: Single

Goals/Motivations: Jane wants to purchase a reliable, fuel-efficient car for her daily commute to and from work. She is looking for a car that is stylish and modern, but also affordable.

Buying Behaviors: Jane is a very practical shopper who prefers to do her research online before making a purchase. She is likely to compare prices and features of cars on various websites and read customer reviews before committing to a purchase. She is also interested in learning more about the environmental impact of the car she chooses.

Pain Points: Jane is concerned about the cost of buying a car and wants to make sure she gets a good deal. She is also worried about the reliability of the car she chooses and wants to make sure she is getting a quality product.

Communication Preferences: Jane prefers to communicate via email or text message, but she is also open to meeting with a salesperson if necessary. She is comfortable using online forms and would prefer to fill out forms on her own time.

Once you have developed your buyer persona, you can use it to create content that is tailored to the needs, interests, and motivations of your target audience.

Additionally, you can use your buyer persona to determine the topics, tone, and format of the content you create, as well as the channels you should use to distribute it.

From the example above, the buyer is concerned with both affordability and reliability. Jane likes to compare prices and features and is interested in the environmental impact.

Knowing this enables you to create content to feed the Content Beast that will resonate with the buyer.

You may create an infographic comparing your brand's car with two competitors' brands.

Or you might create a video on the environmental impact of certain types of cars and how your brand of car approaches this issue. If you are creating some powerful image content, you could focus on how your car is affordable and reliable.

The point is that having the information easily accessible and clearly defined provides you intel that can improve your content and satisfy the Content Beast.

Once you have developed your buyer persona, you can use it to create content that is tailored to the needs, interests, and motivations of your target audience.

Your turn. Let's create a buyer persona for your business. Fill in the following information:

BUYER PERSONA

Name: _________________
Age: _________________
Location: _________________
Occupation: _________________
Income: _________________
Family: _________________

Goals/Motivations:

____
____
____

Buying Behaviors:

____
____
____

Pain Points:

____
____
____

Communication Preferences:

____

NOTE: For a copy of the PDF and other companion tools go to thecontentbeast.co.

PART 3

WHAT TO FEED THE CONTENT BEAST

Content is the atomic particle
of all marketing.
- Rebecca Lieb

Now that you have a clear understanding of who you are really feeding, it is time to shift our attention to the actual type of content to feed the Content Beast. This will be informed by your knowledge of your audience and the variety of content you want to use.

The ultimate goal is to feed the Content Beast – relevant, valuable and consistent content.

Even so, you may find it a bit overwhelming when thinking about where to start and sorting through all the different types of content you could create.

Types Of Content

Here is a starting list of different types of content to feed the Content Beast with pros and cons as well as use cases for each type of content.

Blog Posts

Pros – Easy to create, can be used to establish thought leadership and provide fresh content for Search Engine Optimization (SEO) purposes.

Cons – Can take time to write quality posts and may not always have immediate impact on sales or conversions.

Use Case – Establish yourself as an authority in your industry by providing helpful advice related to the services you offer.

Video

Pros – Highly engaging, shareable, and excellent for demonstrating products or services quickly and effectively.

Cons – Takes more time than other types of content creation (i.e., writing a blog post), requires specialized equipment/software, and hosting costs may apply, depending on how you deliver the video(s).

Use Case – Demonstrate complex processes or products through visual storytelling that helps viewers better understand what is being presented faster than text- based explanations can do alone.

Infographics

Pros – Combines data with visuals, which allows readers to digest information quickly and easily; also, highly shareable across social media platforms due to its attractive design elements.

Cons – Requires more time up front in order to properly research data points needed for the infographic; it must also be designed well in order for it to be effective at conveying messages clearly without becoming too cluttered with information overload.

Use Case – Present complicated topics such as market trends or product features in an easy-to-understand format that appeals visually while still providing important facts/ details within a single image file type such as JPEG or PNG or PDF formats.

eBooks/Whitepapers

Pros – High value content that provides readers with detailed information about a particular topic; often seen as an authoritative source due their lengthier form of writing compared with shorter blog posts.

Cons – Takes longer amount of time from start to finish compared with other forms of content marketing like videos or infographics; requires considerable research into the topic before any actual writing begins.

Use Case – Generate leads by offering whitepapers/eBooks behind gated landing pages where visitors must submit their contact info before downloading them.

Podcasts

Pros – Easy way for brands and businesses alike to connect directly with their audience via audio recordings shared online through various podcast networks (iTunes, Spotify etc.); great way for busy professionals who don't have much free time but want access to valuable insights offered by experts within their field.

Cons – Hosting fees may apply depending upon chosen platform; editing and production costs could become expensive if done professionally.

Use Cases – Educate listeners on specific topics related directly to business goals while building relationships between hosts and guests featured on shows.

Evergreen Vs. Fresh Cut Content™

Evergreen content refers to content that remains relevant and valuable over an extended period. It is not time-sensitive and can be useful to your audience regardless of when they access it.

Evergreen content tends to address timeless topics, concepts, or issues that continue to be of interest to the target audience.

It can also refer to items that remain the same over time.

The power of evergreen content is that you can create and schedule it ahead of time.

As a fan of quotations, I consistently share famous quotes (like I do in this book). The quotes I share are ones that have been established. A Ben Franklin quote isn't going to change (even if there is some debate if he really said a particular one).

Valentine's Day comes every year on February 14th. It is highly unlikely to change.

Facts that are fixed represent another example of evergreen content.

The date of the first landing on the moon isn't going to change.

Creating evergreen content is essential to a sound content marketing strategy. It enables you to feed the Content

Beast in a systematic way as these pieces of content will remain constant over time.

On the other hand, Fresh Cut Content™ is timely and relevant for a specific period. It focuses on current events, trends, or topics that have immediate significance. This type of content quickly loses relevance as time passes.

Here's an example of related content that shows the difference between evergreen and Fresh Cut Content™.

Poker legend, Doyle "Texas Dolly" Brunson won the World Series of Poker Main Event in May 1976 and then again in May 1977.

The fact that Brunson won back-to-back championships is evergreen. It won't change, and you could share this information at any time, and if you are a poker fan, it would still be relevant.

Sadly, on May 14, 2023, Brunson passed away. This news was of significance at the time of his passing, and while the event is fixed in time, the relevance of this event mattered at the time, which would deem it Fresh Cut Content™.

The key distinction between evergreen content and Fresh Cut Content™ lies in their longevity and relevance. Evergreen content has enduring value, while Fresh Cut Content™ is time-sensitive and loses relevance as events unfold or trends change.

Newsflash: You need **BOTH** evergreen and Fresh Cut Content™.

The most powerful person in the
world is the storyteller.
- Steve Jobs

The Real Power Of Story

I'd like to tell you a story. It took place back in 1918 in the city of Philadelphia, where I grew up. When I've started to tell this story, people have oddly and automatically assumed the story was about me. While I do have more than my fair share of gray hair, I'm not *that* old.

This story is about a young man named Charles, who is graduating from Central High School. Charles is an exceptional math student. He's the top student at his high school and one of the top math minds in the city, if not that state.

Charles is offered multiple full-ride scholarships to attend engineering school.

Unfortunately for Charles, his family is very poor. They cannot afford for Charles to go to college for *free*! His family needs him to earn money.

As such, instead of attending college, Charles gets a job at a steel manufacturing factory in northeast Philadelphia. While this job is not engaging in the least to Charles, he does not complain, and he works diligently at the factory day after day.

One day, a friend of Charles named David arrives at work with some books under his arms. When Charles spots him, he asks David,

"What are you doing with those books?"

"I'm going to Temple Law School at night," David replies.

"How much is it?"

"$35 a term."

Now even by 1918 standards, this is not a lot of money. It is quite a reasonable amount.

Charles thinks about this opportunity. Although he had not intended to pursue law, he thinks it would certainly be an improvement over his factory work.

Charles applies for admission to Temple University Law School and is required to take an entrance exam. He is accepted, despite never having attended an undergraduate program.

Clearly this is not possible now, but back in 1918 neither a college degree nor a high LSAT score appeared to be prerequisites for law school admission.

Charles continues to work at the factory while he attends law school at night and four years later, he obtains his Juris Doctor degree. Finally, he is able to leave his factory job.

Charles works as an attorney in different capacities over the next 12 or so years, and it becomes clear he has the intellectual chops to excel in this profession.

In 1934 at the ripe age of 34 Charles makes history – at least Pennsylvania legal history. Charles becomes the youngest attorney in the history of Pennsylvania to become a judge.

This is an incredible achievement, and Charles goes on to have an illustrious judicial career for more than 50 years as a respected judge.

Charles' record stands for nearly 40 years, until his very own son Richard breaks it at the age of 32.

While I attended law school myself, graduating from Temple Law School, I did not follow in the footsteps of my grandfather, Charles, or my father, Richard. In fact, I did not pursue a career in law at all. That's another story for another time.

If I wanted to share the facts about my proud family history, I could have simply stated that my father and grandfather were judges.

Those are the facts.

I believe that the likelihood of you remembering these facts, however, is much greater due to the way I shared that information – through a story.

As described earlier, we are suffering from short atten-tion spans, and brands are constantly battling for the attention of their audience.

In addition, we are all suffering from infobesity with the incredible volume of content bombarding consumers each day, every day.

How can marketers help brands possibly stand out in this overwhelming sea of content?

The answer may surprise you. It is not some fancy, new technology developed to penetrate the human mind.

In fact, the solution to connecting your message with your audience dates back 30,000 years!

Story.

From the early Chauvet Cave drawings, human beings have been utilizing the power of story to effectively communicate.

In fact, for many of us this may seem obvious. After all, we've been telling stories since we were young.

It appears, however, that as we grow older, we find our communication shifts to a more data-driven, informational approach. At least, this is true in many businesses.

When I share my belief that story is the best way to connect your message to your audience – I am often met with nodding heads, indicating a minimum understanding of the concept.

If you consider the story of my family legacy, many would agree that the story resonates more than the mere facts.

I am certainly not the only one promoting the use of storytelling for business communication.

The Content Beast loves a good story – as its favorite form of content, stories are the most satisfying, nutritious and delicious content it consumes.

What I love about my passion for using what I refer to as StoryContent™ to improve communication is that there is a scientific basis for this belief. I often say – "Story Matters. Science proves it."

The Science Of Story

While at Princeton University, neuroscientist Uri Hasson, was fascinated by how a person's brain behaved depending on the type of communication it consumed. His study led to the conclusion that effective communication is all about brain chemistry.

He conducted an experiment to explore the difference in brain activity depending on the stimulus or input that a person receives.

There were two groups – or two audiences.

The first group was given incredible amounts of data. Facts and figures galore - often related to how brands share features and benefits of their product or service.

Unfortunately, this is often how presenters internally and externally share information with participants. They jam their PowerPoint presentations with as much content as possible, typically with more bullets than a saloon in the wild west. The result is often what some refer to as "Death by PowerPoint"!

The brain activity of this group was intriguing. Two primary parts of the brain activated – the Broca's and Wernick's areas.

These two parts of our brains are critically important. They enable us to understand the meaning of the information that is shared. Without these parts of the brain activating, we would not be able to comprehend the content provided.

The brain activity of the second group, those that were told a story that incorporated the information, was VERY different.

The Broca's and Wernick's areas activated – which was good – as the people would be able to decode the meaning of the content.

In addition to these parts of the brain, the person's brain lit up with activity. Various parts of the brain activated depending on the nature of the story.

The remarkable thing about the brain activity of those that heard a story was that the parts of their brain that activated were the parts used if they were experiencing the action of the story themselves.

Neural Coupling

What this means is that the audience was vicariously experiencing the story on a neural level. Further, Professor Hasson discovered something incredible – the brain activity of the speaker was mirrored by the brain activity of the listener. He referred to this as neural coupling.

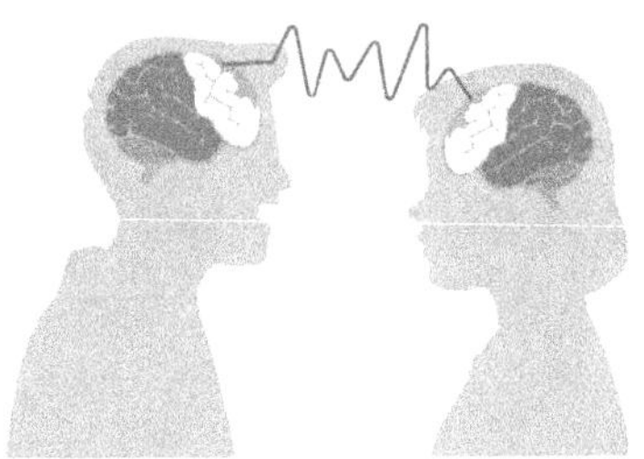

If I were to tell you a story about me kicking a ball – *your* motor cortex would activate. If I told you a story about the sweet smell of fresh-baked chocolate chip cookies, *your* olfactory cortex would activate.

Moreover, among the many hormones that increased in the group that was told a story was an increase in cortisol and oxytocin.

Cortisol is the stress hormone, or the flight or fight hormone.

Why is this so important in connecting your content to your audience? It triggers your attention.

Hopefully, at this stage, we understand the great significance of your content attracting the attention of your audience.

Telling a good story is a pattern interrupt - - one that hooks the listener and brings them into the message you are sharing.

Oxytocin is often referred to as the love hormone. It is frequently associated with pregnancy and birth as a significant element in mother-infant bonding.

As a feel-good hormone, it taps into our emotional state. This increase in feeling good and encouraging bonding will enhance the connection your message can have with the audience. We become more invested in the story and the content being shared.

The results from the experiment showcased a 20-40% increase in both the understanding and retention of the message.

Wouldn't we all like to have our content be better understood and remembered?

And there's more.

According to various websites, "stories are 22 times more memorable than facts alone."

Wow! What a great stat if you are trying to provide some evidence of the power of story.

Sadly, it appears that this claim of stories being that much more memorable is a bit suspect.

When people have attempted to trace the source of this impressive stat – they come up empty.

Despite references to Jerome Bruner's *Actual Minds, Possible Worlds*, which discusses the elements of cognition and narrative, the book never states the actual statistic. Other references to the assertion of stories being more memorable also lead to dead ends.

All is not lost, however. There are two studies, one by Stanford and one by Chip and Dan Heath (authors of *Made to Stick*) that demonstrate that story enhances recall between 7 to 12 times more than facts or data alone.

There are two important points from above. First, don't always assume what you read is 100% accurate. Second, stories do have a powerful role to play in helping an audience connect with the message you are trying to convey.

As such, by feeding the Content Beast StoryContent^{TM} you are advancing your objective – increasing the connection to your audience.

A Word (Or Two) On Viral Content

I often share a meme like the illustration below, where a client or supervisor asks his marketing department or partners:

"If you could just create compelling content that everyone loves…that would be great."

There is no magic wand, fairy dust, or marketing spell that can guarantee that a particular piece of content will *go **viral.***

Nor should that be the goal.

Vanity metrics like follower count do not help you understand your own performance in a way that informs future strategies.

There is a variety of tips and tricks that purport to get more clicks, followers, and engagement that some marketers will swear by – though in most instances when you dig a little deeper, you realize that the promises are quite shallow. (See what I did there?)

It is more important to connect with a smaller, *relevant* group who will engage and hopefully buy from you than a larger group that feigns real interest and moves on.

It is also very difficult to predict what will end up connecting with the zeitgeist at any particular moment, which is why it is important to stick to best practices when feeding the Content Beast.

Corporate Storytelling

While I am pleased that there is a scientific basis for the power of story connected to how human brains are hardwired for story, how this applies to real life is often questioned.

There are many academic studies, which are conducted in specific, controlled circumstances, that do not always transfer to the working world outside academia.

For those that are a bit skeptical of the application of the Science of Story, let me share a few examples of how corporate America has embraced story in fundamental policies and practices.

Motorola

The Motorola organization has hired outside improv performers to train their executives on how to create stories on the fly to boost creativity and understanding of given material.

Proctor & Gamble

The giant that is Proctor & Gamble has engaged Hollywood directors to share how to craft better stories to improve internal communication at the company.

Kimberly-Clark

When executives join Kimberly-Clark, part of their onboarding is a 2-day workshop on crafting stories.

Nike

Nike provides all new executives with a 2-day Corporate Storytelling program as part of its onboarding. Fun fact - for years, Nike has had an executive with the title Chief Storytelling Officer.

3M

My favorite of all is 3M – the company famous for making Post-it notes. A number of years ago, 3M banned bullet points for its executives' presentations. Instead, it provides training on strategic narratives.

Don't you feel better knowing that some big brands have embraced the power of story?

When I share the Science of Story – my aim is to express *WHY* story matters.

Between the science and practice of embracing story, it should be very clear that if you use stories, you will communicate more effectively.

Create A Story Bank

A story bank is a collection of narratives that you can easily draw on when needed. While some may be able to keep all of their stories inside their head, I strongly recommend creating an organized system to access them more efficiently and effectively. Index or tag your stories in order that you or other users can easily retrieve them. This repository of compelling narratives and anecdotes allows you to effortlessly select the right message to connect with your audience.

Leveraging the power of narrative resonance will enable you to feed and captivate the Content Beast, a critical factor in modern business to attract and connect with a company's audience.

Remember, don't look for the perfect story. Take your story and make it perfect.

PART 4

HOW TO FEED THE CONTENT BEAST

Content is anything that adds value
to the reader's life.
- Avinash Kaushik

If you purchased this book, there is a good chance you had an inkling for the need to create valuable and compelling content on a consistent basis to connect with your audience.

By this section of the book, the concept of feeding the Content Beast has hopefully been fully embraced.

That still leaves the very important question of HOW. How does someone create content?

Like any other endeavor where you are looking to create something, we start with *thinking* (I know, a novel concept).

In this concept, what I mean by thinking is the process of IDEATION - coming up with ideas for content.

Let's start with brainstorming.

A brainstorming session is a great way to think and develop ideas for anything. Content creation is no different.

Benefits Of Brainstorming

Brainstorming sessions have numerous benefits, including:

1. **Encourages creativity**
    Brainstorming sessions are designed to stimulate creativity and generate a wide range of ideas. This is done by allowing everyone to contribute and build upon one another's ideas, leading to more innovative and unique ideas.

2. **Generates more ideas**
   Brainstorming sessions can produce a large number of ideas in a short amount of time, which can lead to a wider range of potential solutions or approaches to a problem.

3. **Fosters teamwork and collaboration**
   Brainstorming sessions encourage participation and collaboration, which can help build teamwork and strengthen relationships among team members.

4. **Increases engagement and participation**
   Brainstorming sessions can help to engage team members who may not be as vocal in other settings, giving everyone an equal opportunity to share their thoughts and ideas.

5. **Improves decision making**
   By generating a large number of ideas and considering a range of perspectives, brainstorming sessions can help teams make more informed and effective decisions.

6. **Enhances problem-solving skills**
   Brainstorming sessions can help individuals develop and improve their problem-solving skills by encouraging them to think outside the box and consider different approaches to a problem.

7. **Boosts morale**
   Brainstorming sessions can be fun and energizing, which can help to boost team morale and motivation.

8. **Facilitates innovation**
   Brainstorming sessions can lead to innovative and breakthrough ideas that can help organizations stay competitive and adapt to changing market conditions.

Overall, brainstorming sessions can be a powerful tool for teams and organizations looking to generate new ideas, solve complex problems, and foster collaboration and teamwork.

Get Your Brainstorm On

With all those benefits, let's look at how to actually implement brainstorming. While there are many ways to approach brainstorming, here is a breakdown of the typical steps involved in a brainstorming session, along with a brief description of each step:

1. **Define the problem or goal**
   The first step in a brainstorming session is to clearly define the problem or goal that the team is trying to address. This ensures that everyone is on the same page and understands the scope of the brainstorming session.

2. **Set the rules**
    It's important to establish some ground rules for the brainstorming session, such as encouraging everyone to participate, not criticizing or dismissing ideas, and focusing on quantity over quality.

3. **Generate ideas**
    Once the problem or goal has been defined and the rules have been established, the team can begin generating ideas. This can be done through a variety of methods, such as verbal brainstorming, written lists, or mind maps.
    At this stage there are no bad ideas. The objective is to come up with as many ideas as possible without judgment.

4. **Build on ideas**
    As ideas are generated, the team can start to build on and expand them. This can involve combining ideas, refining them, or exploring different angles or perspectives.

5. **Evaluate and prioritize**
    Once a large number of ideas have been generated, the team can start to evaluate and prioritize them. This can be done based on criteria such as feasibility, impact, or alignment with the overall goal.

6. **Take action**

    Finally, the team can decide on the best course of action based on the ideas that were generated and prioritized. This could involve further research or development, implementation, or additional brainstorming sessions.

Overall, the key to a successful brainstorming session is to encourage open communication, creativity, and collaboration among team members, while staying focused on the problem or goal at hand.

If you fail to plan, you are
planning to fail.
- Benjamin Franklin

Why Did You Rearrange The Furniture?

When I was a teenager, from time to time, my parents would go away and leave my younger brother Alex and me home alone (though it was intentional, unlike the John Hughes film).

This was a golden opportunity for two teenage boys to take advantage of our parents' absence and…host a party.

Our dining room had a sliding door, and we thought we were very clever by taking all the furniture and valuables from the living room and putting them out of harm's way behind the door.

In fact, it worked well, as there were no broken lamps or stained sofas.

The party was a success. The next day Alex and I were feeling pretty good about ourselves as we slid the door back from the dining room and saw all the furniture and breakables safely secured inside.

Our smiles faded as we turned back to the living room and scratched our heads, unsure where things were meant to go.

While we had wrongly assumed that our memory would enable us to replace everything in its original position, we did the best we could.

When our parents returned, Alex and I nervously waited to see if they noticed anything different.

They did.

Our mother asked why we had moved some of the furniture in the living room. Alex and I looked at each other for a brief moment, and I quickly shared that we thought we'd mix it up a bit as a surprise.

Thankfully, she didn't detect how shaky our story was and we survived unscathed.

A few months later, my parents again decided to leave us at home over the weekend – and again we decided to have a small gathering of our closest 100 friends.

This time, however, we decided to make a better plan. While the original plan seemed good, it was a bit half-baked.

This time we prepared. Before moving the furniture and valuables, we created a detailed map of the layout of the living room and where all the items were located.

The day after another successful soiree, we easily returned the house to its previous state, and our parents never knew any better.

The Man With The Content Plan

When it comes to feeding the Content Beast, having a plan will most certainly increase your chances of achieving success with your content objectives.

Without a plan, you may make decisions on the fly or base them on incomplete information.

Further, not having a plan can make you feel anxious, and this can lead to mistakes or missed opportunities, which can ultimately prevent you from creating content that appeases the Content Beast.

With a good content plan, you will stay focused and motivated. You have a playbook that provides a clear understanding of what you need to do to succeed.

It is for this reason that I included the **21-Day Content Marketing Playbook** at the end of this book.

It is the roadmap for sustained success.

The Plan For The Content

While the **21-Day Content Marketing Playbook** will give you the specific steps for overall success, there are some general ideas about creating content to feed the Beast to keep in mind, even if you don't use the playbook.

After you have brainstormed and determined which content to develop, then it's time to start the process of creating the content.

Once you have a piece of content or a collection of content, you will want to **review** that content.

Typically, you would do your own review first, and then it is recommended to have someone else review it.

This could be a team member or trusted advisor. The nature of the content may inform who reviews it.

After reviewing it and identifying anything that needs changing, the next step is to **edit** the content to take that feedback into account.

Once you edit, the content would be **shared** with the ultimate decision-maker for final approval.

Of course, when it goes for final approval, there is a good chance there may be some additional feedback. In this instance, it would go back to the edit stage to incorporate that feedback.

This final process of revisions and approval may take several rounds.

Part of your plan should include how this process will go, who will have what responsibility at what stage, and how many brainstorming rounds you will have.

[Note: While this is typical when working with an outside partner, it is still worth doing even if the process is internal.]

Clear communication and expectations will be critical to having a smooth plan.

The ABCs Of Telling Compelling Stories

As we considered in the section on WHAT type of content to share, hopefully it is clear that StoryContent™ is the Content Beast's favorite dish.

Often when I share the Science of Story and the underlying WHY story matters and how science proves it, most nod in agreement.

As we recognize that we have been using story to effectively communicate with people since we were children, the concept is something we generally agree is powerful. Yes, people say, I get it – story matters. We understand the WHY.

What typically follows is the question, "How do you tell good stories?"

There are a few best practices that we can all implement to tell more compelling stories. Here I share a few in the form of the A, B, and C of telling more compelling stories.

A is for Know Your Audience

While there are many potential A's for telling compelling stories (see below for a pretty good list), for my money it's all about the **Audience!**

Remember the 11th commandment: *Know Thy Audience?* This is still critical to how to tell a compelling story. If you tell a great story to an audience that doesn't resonate with them, then it's not really a great story. A great story is one that connects with the audience – the specific audience you are trying to engage.

Let's get started with your audience.

Write down 9 things you know about your target audience:
1. _______________________________
2. _______________________________
3. _______________________________
4. _______________________________
5. _______________________________
6. _______________________________
7. _______________________________
8. _______________________________
9. _______________________________

Many groups have been asked what the A for telling compelling stories is. Here's a list of some of the other A words to keep in mind when sharing a story:

- Authority
- Adventure
- Action
- Amusing
- Appealing
- Accurate
- Articulate
- Absorbing
- Artful

- Artistic
- Alluring
- Awe-inspiring
- Active
- Approachable
- Attractive
- Atypical

B is for Be Authentic

Many audiences have been asked what the B stands for in telling compelling stories. After hearing a number of responses, I share that the B of compelling stories is to BE AUTHENTIC.

I'll let this land for a moment and then share that in fact, this is a bit inauthentic. To be completely authentic, I have to point out that this tip is really another A – Authentic - more than it is a B for how to Be.

Can you think of a powerful word that starts with B that encapsulates the meaning of authenticity?

If you find a good one, please let me know.

The closest proposed was probably Bona Fide or Believable, though neither captures the sentiment of how important it is to be genuine when sharing stories.

The Consequences Of Being Inauthentic

Despite the widespread idiom of *fake it till you make it*, you must not be inauthentic in your communication – if you try and feed the Content Beast a bunch of BS, it will quickly reject it. Not only will the Content Beast spit out any rubbish you try to feed it, it will become grumpier than it was before you fed it.

This does not mean every story you share has to be 100% accurate down to the color of someone's shoes or the specific place or time of any event. There is certainly room for some poetic license, creative interpretation, and coloring of the message you are sharing.

You can't, however, make stuff up that is clearly misleading, untrue, or fraudulent.

Creating false content can put you in real hot water and in the end is not worth the risk of losing your audience.

It's not simply a bad moral decision; it's also a bad business decision.

By deceiving your audience, you are giving them a bad brand experience. Well, assuming you are caught – which is likely in the modern world we live in.

The consequences of a bad brand experience are catastrophic.

Dissatisfied customers will tell between 9-15 people about their experience. Around 13% of dissatisfied customers tell more than 20 people.

In Ruby Newell-Legner's "Understanding Customers," he states that it takes 12 positive experiences to make up for one unresolved negative experience.

Being authentic is the best practice in telling stories and in business in general.

Often the best place to begin your journey to share authentic stories is to consider YOUR WHY.

Simon Sinek's exceptional book *Start with Why* expresses that we buy WHY someone does what they do rather than WHAT they do.

[Note: To get the broad strokes of starting with why, watch Simon Sinek's incredible TEDx talk.]

Write down – WHY you do what you do:

____

____

____

Here are some additional B words for telling great stories:

- Bona fide
- Believable
- Bold
- Brilliant
- Breathtaking
- Balanced
- Beautiful
- Brief
- Brave
- Beneficia

- Bright
- Big

C is for Connection

C is not for cookie – though who doesn't like a tasty cookie?

When you feed the Content Beast relevant, valuable content, you **connect** with your audience.

This is the ultimate goal of content marketing.

This is also the primary goal of telling compelling stories – connection.

As we talked about earlier, stories have been connecting people since there *were* people. It's the most powerful way to communicate and to connect.

There are two specific ways to increase your connection when it comes to telling stories.

Use Your Senses

The five senses – touch, taste, smell, vision, and hearing - are mighty powerful. We want to leverage them when sharing stories to connect with our audience.

Remember neural coupling? It's worth repeating. When the brain sees or hears a story, its neurons fire in the same patterns as the speaker's brain. Stories synchronize the listener's brain with the teller's brain.

As such, when we use the senses in our storytelling – it is a way to hardwire into the brain activity of your audience.

When we share detailed sensory descriptions in our narrative messages, we connect on a deeper level through shared sensory experiences on a brain activity level.

Emotional Connection

In the same respect, including emotional components in our content enables our audience to also experience that emotional state, which then translates into a deeper connection with the message and the messenger (whether that be a brand or a person).

Think of some of those touching Super Bowl ads that tug at the heartstrings. While they may appear a bit senti-mental and even perhaps manipulative, there is a reason why these advertisers are spending millions of dollars on these types of ads – they work.

We identify on an emotional level, whether it be about friendship (I keep thinking of the horse-puppy rela-tionship of a particular Budweiser commercial), loss, excitement, or whatever other emotion represents our message effectively.

Everything and anything you can do to increase the emotional connection is beneficial to your audience.

How does your customer feel BEFORE they interact with your product or service?

____

____

How does your customer feel AFTER they interact with your product or service?

____

____

What senses are activated when they interact with your brand?

____

____

Additional C words for great stories:

- Captivating
- Character-driven
- Clever
- Complex
- Creative
- Crisp
- Colorful
- Cohesive
- Convincing
- Charming

Bonus Letter For Better Stories – V

Part of good content marketing (and therefore good book writing) is to provide as much value as one can.

The Content Beast, like all of us, loves to have an extra dish – a little bonus treat. Think of it as the whipped cream or cherry on top.

For telling better stories, the cherry on top is the letter V. In fact, some might argue that V is more like an entire dessert.

Ok, now what could possibly be so scrumptious for telling better stories that it's being compared to what we all crave – and that's the point.

V is for…Victory!

Just kidding. Although every time I ask an audience about what the V could stand for, invariably someone shouts out, "Victory!"

In our case, the V stands for **V̲isual.**

Visual stories are indeed the sweet, delicious content that the Content Beast and your audience are craving. It is the type of content that we all eat voraciously and then ask for more.

Video continues to be the visual content of choice as it engages audiences more and more. Whether this is Behind the Scenes (BTS), Testimonials, or Case Studies, or simply recording a selfie video of what you are doing at that moment in time, video is an essential component of content creation.

There are times when you want to invest in a more polished, produced video. Hire those with that expertise. Others times, just grab your iPhone and hit Record. Either way, the point it to start making videos and sharing them with your audience.

There is a lot of scientific research and data that supports why we love visual content.

While a few people jokingly say that 38.9% of statistics are made up (including that one), statistics that are based on sound research and reliable data can be valuable tools for understanding concepts – like the power of visual communication.

Here are just a few statistics that can be used as further evidence of the critical importance of visual communication:

- The human brain processes visual information 60,000 times faster than text.
- 90% of the information processed by the brain is visual.
- It takes only 13 milliseconds for the human brain to process an image.
  - To put that in perspective, it takes you 300 to 400 milliseconds to blink your eye, which is 1/3 of a second. This means that your brain can identify what it's looking at approximately 30 times faster than you can blink your eye!
- Visual content improves learning and the retention of knowledge by 400%.

Let's do a little exercise to demonstrate the power of visual communication.

See how long it takes you to identify the following movies, only using graphics:

You should hopefully have been able to identify them fairly easily.

The point being that a variety of visual storytelling is the best content to feed the Content Beast to keep him happy and is also a sure-fire way to capture your audience's attention.

List three pieces of visual content you could create to showcase how you help your customers:

1. _______________________________________
2. _______________________________________
3. _______________________________________

Other V words for leveraging the power of story:

- Valuable
- Vivid
- Versatile
- Visceral
- Visionary
- Virtuous
- Vibrant
- Valiant
- Vast
- Vital
- Vulnerable

StoryContent™ Structure

One of the challenges of feeding the Content Beast is how to organize the broader content plan and the particular pieces of content.

What are the basic principles of how to structure StoryContent™?

Thankfully, someone has already answered this question for us.

The Godfather Of Narrative

Who is the Godfather of narrative? I've heard a number of reasonable answers when this question is posed.

Dickens?

Joseph Campbell?

Tolkien?

Spielberg?

There are many titans of literature, theater, film, etc.

Yet, I think we need to go back...way back to about 350 B.C. to discover the foundation of narrative structure and the person I jokingly refer to as the Godfather of narrative: Aristotle.

Aristotle: Jeopardy Champ

Aristotle's three-act structure is a dramatic structure used in storytelling that dates back to ancient Greece. Aristotle was a philosopher and literary critic who wrote extensively on the art of storytelling in his work *Poetics*, in which he laid out the key components of drama and the structure of a successful play.

Among Aristotle's many accomplishments, one that is not as well known is that he was, in fact, a Jeopardy champion!

His final Jeopardy category that catapulted him to victory was:

STORY CHARACTERS

The answer was:

THIS CHARACTER NEEDS TO BE IN EVERY STORY

There were many characters considered from protagonist to the villain to even a narrator. While these are important characters in a compelling story Aristotle, being the clever fellow that he was, knew the correct question:

Who is BIG MAN ED?

Although this baffled most people, it was the right response. Big Man Ed is a simple character in almost every effective story.

Ok, we are being a bit cute with this answer, as Big Man Ed represents not a specific person per se, but instead illustrates a concept.

Big Man Ed stands for the elements of any well-structured story – which is the foundation of Aristotle's three-act structure.

It is based on the idea that a well-constructed story should have a **Beginning, a Middle, and an End**, with each part serving a specific purpose in advancing the plot and building tension.

As such, Big Man Ed is a mnemonic device to remember the importance of having a beginning, a middle, and an end for every story.

Vonnegut's Shapes Of Stories

In terms of a well-crafted story, novelist Kurt Vonnegut provides a starting point for understanding the mechanics of structure.

Ironically, this brilliant contribution to powerful narratives does not come from any of his popular novels. Instead, it is the output of his rejected master's thesis in anthropology.

Vonnegut's thesis was that every story can be plotted on a grid and that there are a finite number of what he called shapes of stories.

The vertical y-axis of the graph had good fortune on the top and ill fortune on the bottom.

On the horizontal x-axis, the left side was the beginning of the story, while the right side represented the end (see graphic below).

Man In Hole

Vonnegut plotted eight different stories. Let's consider one:

Man in Hole (though, as Vonnegut shared, it needn't be about a man and it needn't be about a hole.)

It's about a person whose life is going along OK until some action occurs and it brings him down into this hole of misfortune.

He stays there until some other action takes him back out of the hole to a better place from where he even started.

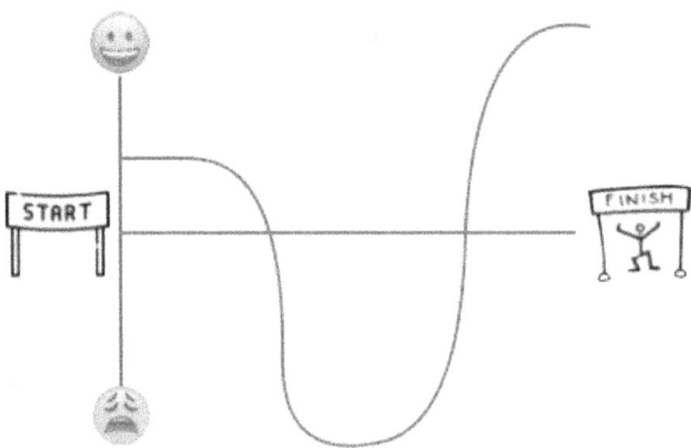

Vonnegut's shapes of stories provide a framework for how we can start to tell stories that have a shape and a universal theme. We can then shade in those shapes with personal details and provide that color in context and authenticity.

The Story P.A.D.

Most people are at least a little familiar with the three-act structure as it is prevalent in books, movies, plays, and any other narrative that is generally consumed by society at large.

Therefore, I find many people accept this axiom of good storytelling – though they always seem to ask the same question:

What should the beginning, middle, and end of my story be?

As we are considering this in the context of feeding the Content Beast, the beginning, middle, and end need to effectively share the story of a business while remaining customer/audience focused.

As noted earlier, Big Man Ed – the concept for this construct - is a bit simple.

Consequently, we needed to craft a formula that even his simple self could understand and implement.

Enter **THE STORY P.A.D.** – a simple and easy-to-use formula to create any business story.

The P.A.D. represents the beginning, middle, and end of your business story.

We start with P. The P stands for the **problem** or **pain** of your customer. It is important to start with your customers in mind in order to capture their attention. As noted earlier, your audience wants to know what's in it for them.

By having the beginning of the story address their issue, you immediately focus on them.

It also helps prequalify your audience. If you share a message that starts with a problem – those that don't have that problem will move on and not engage. The result is that the content is **relevant** - a key component of how you effectively feed the Content Beast.

The A stands for the **answer** to the problem of your customer. It is the solution that your product or service provides.

This enables you to connect your customers' needs with your ability to satisfy them. It is the **value** required to engage them and again fulfills another critical element of how you can successfully feed the Content Beast.

Many marketers and businesses stop there. They state the problem of their customer and then show them their solution that will cure it.

The end of the story, however, can be the closer - the one that takes them from only interested to a paying customer.

The D of the Story P.A.D. represents the **difference** that the customer will experience in their life or business. It is the impact or the transformation that will occur as a result of using your product or service. This paints the picture of a better, happier life due to engaging with your brand.

Vonnegut's Man in Hole shape of a story is a really good shape for businesses to tell their story, and it actually aligns with the Story P.A.D. The man is the customer who has some sort of problem or pain that takes them down into this hole of misfortune.

Then your product or service provides the answer that brings them out of the hole, and it makes a difference in their life and brings them even further up from where they started.

Let's consider a couple examples of the Story P.A.D.

While I am not a fan of the stereotypical ambulance-chasing attorneys, personal injury firms do a very good job using the Story P.A.D. to feed the Content Beast.

P – Problem/Pain

Have you been injured in an accident?

This gets to the root of your audience's issue right away.

If you haven't been in an accident, you will simply ignore this content. If you or someone you know *has* been in an accident, your ears will prick up, as it most likely is on your mind.

A - Answer

The law firm of Grunfeld & Smith can provide sound legal guidance to promptly address your injuries.

D - Difference

You will be made whole again through compensation for your pain and suffering.

This simple formula can be applied to almost any business.

Here are two other quick examples:

Tax Services

P - Problem/Pain

Is your business behind in preparing its taxes, and are you frustrated by the process?

A - Answer

Contact the tax consultancy Kirk and Taylor, experts at helping small businesses prepare their taxes.

D - Difference

You can relax knowing your taxes will be filed appropriately and that you can expect a tax refund.

Garage Doors

P – Problem/Pain

Is your garage door damaged? Are you stuck outside your garage?

A – Answer

Door Doctors can help with its expert door service, providing repairs and new installations.

D – Difference

You'll be able to access your home easily and even check if your doors are open or closed remotely.

While these examples may seem simplistic, it is that simplicity that makes them so effective.

With diminishing attention spans and infobesity, feeding the Content Beast, simple, easy-to-digest content is the shortest distance to connecting with your audience.

Your turn. Fill in the blanks for your business's Story P.A.D.

P – Problem/Pain

The Pain or problem of my customer is

____

____

____

A - Answer

The Answer or solution our product or services provide is

____

____

____

D – Difference

The difference or impact it makes in the lives or businesses is

____

____

____

The Story P.A.D. formula can help you easily generate winning StoryContent™ to feed the Content Beast.

Sharing Is Caring: DISTRIBUTION

You've worked hard up to this point on the challenge of creating consistent, valuable content for your target audience.

You've spent time learning about your audience.

You've considered the variety of content that will resonate best with your audience.

You have even embraced the true power of using story to develop a variety of tasty, compelling StoryContent™ to feed the Content Beast.

Now what?

It's time to SHARE your content!

I'm reminded of the concept of the tree in the forest. If a tree falls in the woods and no one is there to hear it – does it make a sound?

While I am not sure what the best answer is to *that* existential question, what I do know is that if you spend a good deal of time getting to know your audience, developing dynamic, relevant, valuable content, but you never share it with anyone – it will NOT have any particular impact. It will likely be a waste of effort.

The Perfection Trap

Often in the creative process, there are those who are perfectionists and want to make sure everything is just right before sharing.

While it is very important to have QUALITY, be careful it doesn't stymie you into not taking any action.

Be mindful of the French proverb most commonly attributed to Voltaire, the famous French writer and activist, that roughly translates to:

PERFECTION IS THE ENEMY OF THE GOOD

Slight variations include Perfection is the Enemy of Progress or the Done.

This means that people who are striving for perfection are actually their own worst enemy.

They're so busy trying to make everything perfect - looking for the best - they don't notice when progress might make a bigger difference than perfection.

Imperfect Action

It is critical to take imperfect action and recognize you could always edit or tweak a bit more.

Sometimes good enough is good enough (again, it does have to be GOOD!)

While my aim is to write a great book that brings you great value, if I kept editing and editing until it was perfect – you wouldn't be reading this. No one would, because it would never be perfect and hence never done.

Feel The Fear...And Do It Anyway

While studying abroad in Sydney, Australia, my closest friends on the program, Donny and Brian, suggest we take an excursion to visit the nearby and beautiful Blue Mountains National Park.

It sounds like a great idea, that is until they mention the *adventure* they wanted to partake there - - abseiling!

I am not familiar with the term *abseiling*, which on this side of the world is called rappelling.

While I don't always share this – I have a fear of heights, especially when open to the elements. This fear is usually contained and I simply avoid situations where I might encounter extreme heights – like rappelling down a cliff!

Against my better judgment, I agree to go on the High and Wild Australian Adventure. It is safe, right? It's not like I am in a foreign country with some ragtag, thrill-seeking adventure group of Australians who are often known for taking needlessly dangerous risks. Oh wait, that's exactly what I am doing.

We gear up with ropes, harnesses, and helmets and are given cursory instructions. The main direction is to lean back. Hmm...not sure I like the sound of that.

Our first abseil is off a 5-meter boulder (only about 15 feet). I figure I could jump down and survive without much incident.

The next abseil is 25 meters (about 80 feet). Looking down through the trees, it is clear a fall from this height would end badly.

Despite my nerves, I manage this height without much panic. We do this height a couple times.

Then we walk a bit to the final spot - - 75 meters (250 feet) or 20 stories down. To make it even better, it is an overhang.

The previous abseils we rappelled with our feet out on the side of the mountain..

This time, I will be leaning back over a cliff, and when I do so, I will then be dangling by the rope in the air.

My heartbeat speeds up. I start to sweat. Panic is now palpable. I do not want to do this.

My guide, Zoltan, is doing his best to calm me and assure me it's all going to be OK.

As he turns, I notice the back of his branded shirt and the slogan of High and Wild Australia Adventures:

Feel the fear… but do it anyway!

Deep breath. Lean back.

As I make my way down, I stop high above the ground. I look out and admire a truly spectacular vista. It is incredible.

Content marketing can sometimes feel scary. I recommend you take a deep breath, lean back, and admire the views. (See what I did there?)

When And Where To Share?

After you accept that your content does not need to be perfect and you need to simply embrace the fear of starting, it's time for you to determine the best place to distribute your content.

This should be informed by how well you know your audience. If you have done the work to *Know Thy Audience*, this should include where and when they spend their time and attention.

You need to decide whether to focus more on traditional media (radio, TV, out of home) or digital (paid search, social, etc.), which again should be informed by your understanding of your audience.

Then within the different options, platforms, and channels, where your audience is most likely to be and to see your content.

If you are trying to reach a B2B audience, LinkedIn is likely a better channel than TikTok. If you are trying to reach a younger audience, then Facebook may not be the best channel to distribute your content.

What platforms do you think your audience uses most?

- Facebook
- Instagram
- YouTube
- LinkedIn

- TikTok
- Pinterest
- Twitter (recently rebranded as X)

In addition, look for ways to leverage other people's audiences. This could be by guest blogging, being a guest on someone else's podcast, or partnering with someone to have them share an email blast promoting your business.

Focus On One Or Two Channels

Some marketing pundits suggest you share content across **ALL** social media platforms. And while you are at it, share through traditional media as well.

This may be unrealistic for most, unless you have a robust team at your disposal. Even so, being on every platform is not the goal. The objective to is to share where those that matter most will be.

It's better to be consistent on a couple platforms than inconsistent on many.

If you focus on a couple platforms – the ones you identify as being most relevant to your audience – you will not only start to master that platform, you will have more engagement.

Organic vs. Paid Digital Content Marketing

When it comes to distributing your content to connect with your audience in the digital space, you need to determine if you are going to do so with organic or paid marketing.

Paid content marketing refers to the practice of promoting content through paid advertising, such as Google Ads, social media ads, or display ads.

It involves paying to have your content seen by a wider audience, often through targeted advertising, with the goal of generating immediate results such as website traffic, leads, or sales.

Organic content marketing, on the other hand, refers to the practice of creating and sharing valuable, informative, and engaging content with the goal of attracting and retaining an audience over time.

This content is distributed through channels such as a blog, social media, or email marketing, and relies on SEO and social media engagement to generate traffic and leads.

Unlike paid content marketing, organic content marketing is free, but it requires a significant investment of time and resources to create high-quality content that resonates with your target audience.

Let's consider the pros and cons of each type a bit more.

Organic Content Marketing

Pros

- Cost-effective
- Builds long-term trust and credibility
- Sustainable results

Cons

- Requires significant investment of time and effort
- Results can take time
- Limited control over distribution

Paid Content Marketing

Pros

- Greater control over targeting and distribution
- Faster results
- Ability to scale

Cons

- Can be expensive
- Requires ongoing investment
- Requires expertise

While it depends on your budget, resources, and objectives, ultimately, it's beneficial to use a combination of both to get the best results whether you use traditional or digital media.

Speaking of media, here is a quick and helpful list of both traditional and digital media where you can distribute your content:

Traditional Media	Digital Media
• Newspapers	• Social Media Platforms
• Direct Mail	• Blogging Platforms
• Magazines	• Email
• Television	• Online Video Platforms
• Radio	• Podcasting Platforms
• Outdoor advertising	• Earned media (PR)

Repurpose With Purpose

Repurposing content refers to taking existing content and transforming it into different formats or repackaging it to reach a new audience. Here are some benefits of repurposing content:

Expanded Reach

Repurposing content allows you to reach a wider audience across different channels and platforms. By adapting content to formats--such as blog posts, videos, infographics, podcasts, or social media posts--you can engage with audiences who prefer different types of content consumption.

Improved SEO and Traffic

Repurposing content gives you an opportunity to optimize it for different keywords, increasing its visibility in search engines. This can drive more organic traffic to your website or other platforms where the repurposed content is published.

Increased Engagement

Different people have different preferences when it comes to consuming content. Repurposing content into various formats enables you to cater to those preferences, leading to increased engagement. Some may prefer reading blog posts, while others may enjoy watching videos or listening to podcasts.

Time and Resource Efficiency

Repurposing content allows you to maximize the value of your existing content assets. Instead of starting from scratch each time, you can leverage the research, ideas, and insights from previous content, saving time and resources in content creation.

Now, let's explore a clear method for effectively repurposing content:

Audit Existing Content

Begin by assessing your existing content library. Identify high-performing content or pieces that have the potential to be repurposed for different formats or channels.

Play the Hits

Recently, I had the good fortune to find myself in a cafe chatting with Anne Schiffmann, a social media expert and author of *Simple Social Media.*

She shared the story of her dad, Bill Figenshu, a very successful, retired radio guy. He was the head of Viacom's radio division and launched some of the most successful radio stations of all time. Annie shared one of his secrets: "Play the hits."

As Annie explained, her dad is a firm believer in finding what works and giving it to your audience.

We often feel pressure to come up with new ideas for content all the time. This isn't the case.

You can take content from before and repurpose it. It's like when an artist releases a greatest hits album.

Queen's greatest hits compilation released in October of 1981, turned out to be one of the bestselling albums of all time. With hits like *Bohemian Rhapsody*, *We Will Rock You* and *Somebody to Love*, Queen's greatest hits record sold 20.6 million certified copies.

This is a powerful strategy you can apply to your content to feed the Content Beast his favorite meals!

You can just take content from three months ago, or six months ago, or a year and share it again.

Remember, your content is aimed at what your audience wants.

When you go to a Taylor Swift concert, you may hear a couple new songs, but the majority of the songs in the show are ones you already know and love. That's why you go to the concert – to hear the music (content) you want.

When you're creating content to feed the Content Beast--yes, new concepts are worthwhile--more important, though, is to repurpose your best content. Change up the visuals, adjust the copy, update the format. Or not.

Just play it again.

Play the hits.

Identify Repurposing Opportunities

Analyze your target audience and the platforms they engage with. Determine which content formats and channels would resonate best with your audience. For example, if your audience is active on YouTube, consider repurposing blog posts into video content.

Choose the Right Format

Based on the identified opportunities, select the appropriate content format for repurposing. It could be converting a long-form article into an infographic, transforming a webinar into a podcast episode, or creating social media posts from key points within a blog post.

Optimize for the New Format

Adapt the content to suit the chosen format. For example, when converting a blog post into a video, you may need to write a script, create visuals, and record or animate the content. Optimize the repurposed content for the platform's requirements and audience preferences.

Promote Across Channels

Once the repurposed content is ready, promote it across relevant channels. Leverage social media, email newsletters, or your website to drive traffic to the repurposed content. Encourage engagement and sharing to extend its reach even further.

Measure and Iterate

Monitor the performance of the repurposed content across different channels and formats. Analyze metrics such as engagement, traffic, conversions, and feedback. Use these insights to refine your repurposing strategy and make improvements for future content repurposing efforts.

By following this method, you can effectively repurpose content, reach new audiences, and maximize the value of your existing content assets. Remember to be strategic, tailor content to each format, and leverage the strengths of each platform to engage with your target audience effectively.

Will The Machines Take Over?

AI (artificial intelligence) is not a new phenomenon.

It has been around for quite a while, and in fact many people use AI every day without realizing it.

Consider Netflix.

Netflix's recommendation system is powered by AI algorithms that analyze user behavior, viewing history, and preferences.

This data is combined with machine learning techniques to provide personalized content recommendations to each user.

The recommendation system takes into account factors such as genre preferences, similar viewing patterns of other users, and content ratings to suggest relevant TV shows and movies.

Or Amazon.

Amazon's recommendation engine is also powered by AI algorithms in the same way.

Have you used the chat feature on a website? These chatbots have become commonplace, providing customer support, answering inquiries, and performing tasks.

These AI-powered systems utilize natural language processing and machine learning to understand and respond to user queries, improving customer service and reducing response times.

Have you asked Alexa, Google, or Siri anything recently?

These voice assistants engage with users in a more natural and human-like manner.

Why is it that in recent times some people have raised grave concerns about AI and its impact on society?

The meteoric rise of AI-powered tool ChatGPT (Generative Pre-Trained Transformer) by OpenAI has brought a lot of these fears to the forefront.

On one hand, people are worried about how people will use and/or *abuse* this powerful technology.

On the other hand, others are hailing the access to the AI tool as a game changer for all types of jobs we humans used to do.

As OpenAI cofounder Greg Brockman shares in his TED talk "Now, these systems, they're not perfect. You cannot overly rely on them." One can use "ChatGPT as a brainstorming partner."

He admits that to get "AI right is going to require participation from everyone. And that's for deciding how we want it to slot in, that's for setting the rules of the road, for what an AI will and won't do."

AI is evolving quickly. It will continue to get better.

OpenAI's mission of "ensuring that artificial general intelligence benefits all of humanity" is admirable. Like any new technology, it is neither good or bad, but who and how it is used will determine that.

A deeper discussion of its moral, ethical, and political implications will be left to others. From my perspective, what is its impact specifically on content marketing?

Does AI Help Feed The Content Beast?

It can certainly assist, though some fear it will replace their jobs.

I tend to agree with the sentiment that we are not going to lose our job to AI. Instead we may lose our job to someone using AI.

Everyone is jumping on the bandwagon of AI and trying to find how it can be used to increase productivity.

After reading multiple articles and listening to many opinions, my perspective is that AI, like other technological advances, will serve as a tool that will make certain jobs much faster and even eliminate certain tasks, in the same way other technology has done. I think AI will work to enhance, not replace human content development.

Consider the following personal story.

I'm an eighth-grader, and I have a biology quiz in the afternoon. There is another section of eighth-grade biology that takes the quiz in the morning.

A few other students and I arrive at class a bit early. The teacher is not there, though on her desk is the pile of quizzes from the earlier class. On the top we see the multiple-choice answers from a fellow student, Sarah.

We all look at each other and quickly jot down the answers to the quiz and take our seats (not my proudest moment).

The teacher and the rest of the class shuffle in, and the teacher hands out the quiz.

As I begin, something funny happens. I compare Sarah's answers with the choices available, and there is a disconnect.

You see, I am prepared for the quiz. I did the work. After reviewing a given question, I know the right answer, and it isn't any of the ones from Sarah's quiz.

As such, I answer according to my own knowledge of the material.

The other students blindly copy Sarah's answers without another thought.

Sarah receives a D on the quiz!

Obviously, the other students also receive Ds for the quiz. [For those that are curious, I got an A!]

The lesson here is don't rely on information you *think* is correct. My classmates all assumed Sarah had the right answers, and we all know what happens when you assume.

My suggestion is to treat AI accordingly. Fact check, double-check and use your own skills, talent, experience, and knowledge to provide the *right* answers.

With ChatGPT, sometimes the questions are more important than the answers.

I'm a fan of the new job that will emerge, the Prompt Engineer. This is a big part of the AI system. You need to ask it good questions to elicit useful answers, and the ability to do so will be in high demand.

Consider some of the findings from a recent survey by resumebuilder.com:

- 90% of companies that are currently hiring want workers with ChatGPT experience
- 29% are looking to hire prompt engineers
- 66% of business leaders say hiring ChatGPT experienced workers will give the company a competitive edge

All of this has led me to think about my own three kids and how they should be spending less time on TikTok and more time on ChatGPT.

Having played with the tool myself, it has certainly helped brainstorm ideas (some even made it into this book).

Here is a list of 9 ways AI can help with content marketing (generated by ChatGPT):

1. **Content Generation**
   AI can generate content by analyzing existing data, trends, and user preferences.

2. **Content Curation**
   AI algorithms can scan and analyze vast amounts of content to curate personalized recommendations for users.

3. **Audience Segmentation**
   AI can analyze user data, demographics, and behavior patterns to segment audiences accurately.

4. **Sentiment Analysis**
   AI-powered sentiment analysis tools can analyze social media posts, reviews, and comments to understand the sentiment and opinions of users toward a brand, product, or topic.

5. **SEO Optimization**
   AI can analyze SEO data and provide insights to improve website rankings and content visibility.

6. **Personalized Recommendations**
   AI algorithms can analyze user data and behavior to deliver personalized content recommendations.

7. **Social Media Management**
   AI can help automate social media management tasks such as scheduling posts, analyzing

engagement metrics, and suggesting content ideas.

8. **Chatbots and Virtual Assistants**
   AI-powered chatbots and virtual assistants can engage with customers, answer frequently asked questions, and provide personalized recommendations.

9. **Social Listening**
   AI-powered tools can monitor social media platforms and online conversations to track brand mentions, sentiment, and customer feedback.

As AI technology continues to advance, it opens up new possibilities and opportunities for marketers to create, optimize, and deliver highly effective content strategies.

You can't improve what you
don't measure.
- Peter Drucker

The Great Experiment

I often relay to people that content marketing (and marketing in general) is part art and part science.

The science part requires you to experiment.

You need to have a clear idea of your objectives – what you are trying to achieve.

And – not to sound like a broken record – you need clarity on who your audience is and what matters to them.

ERA

ERA is an acronym for a process of continually striving to improve your content marketing efforts.

E - Experiment

Within the context of your objective and audience, your content marketing approach should **experiment** with the following:

- Types of content
- Elements of that content (text, image, etc.)
- Variations of content
- When you share
- Where you share
- How often you share
- Segments of whom you share with

R – Review

Once you conduct any experiment, it is critical to **review** your results.

What worked? What didn't work?

You may think you know which of your content performed well – and you may or may not be correct.

It is essential that you measure how well (or not so well) your experiment went, and this is why it is necessary to establish objectives. It is also essential that you determine the metrics you will use to measure performance.

What are the KPIs (Key Performance Indicators) you will use to gauge how successful the content was?

A - Adjust

Assessing the strength of your content in the context of the experiment is vital. If you don't take the next step in making the adjustments to improve it, you've wasted effort.

In order to **improve** your content marketing, you need to review the data points and turn them into actionable insights. Finally, you need to implement these insights.

There is no magic dust to make content viral (and that shouldn't necessarily be the goal). By being thoughtful and using the process of **Experiment, Review, and Adjust,** you can take action to make your efforts more effective as you continually improve.

The journey of a thousand miles
begins with a single step.
- Lao Tzu

The Happy Content Beast

Having a strong content marketing strategy and creating relevant, useful content is not easy, and it does require work.

My hope is that this book has provided a framework to begin.

Let's start now and build one step at a time.

Using the tools and techniques in this book will increase brand awareness and visibility, as well as improve customer engagement and foster deeper relationships.

All of this will enhance lead generation and conversion. As a result, your business will grow and flourish.

Once you successfully feed the Content Beast, your business will thank you as it turns the once angry, hungry beast into a calm, happy and contented creature.

Epilogue

January 24, 1975. Köln, Germany.

It's raining.

A sold-out audience of 1,400 people fill the Köln Opera House. Anticipation fills the air as the audience eagerly awaits the concert from Keith Jarrett, a renowned jazz pianist.

Vera Brandes, Germany's youngest concert promoter, is filled with something quite different: panic.

Vera has organized this very ambitious concert. At only 18, she is a passionate advocate for Jarrett's music and recognizes the impact he could have on the German audience. In her initial efforts to convince Jarrett to come and perform in Germany, Brandes reaches out to him, expressing her admiration for his talent and sharing her vision for a memorable concert experience.

Vera's persistence and genuine belief in Jarrett's artistic brilliance are instrumental in convincing him to take a leap of faith and bring his exceptional talent to Germany.

Unfortunately, things do not go smoothly.

Knowing Jarrett's reputation of his high standards and dedication to his craft, Brandes works tirelessly to secure a suitable venue for the concert.

The concert takes place on a Friday at the late hour of 11:30 pm, following an earlier opera performance. The late time is the only one the administration would make available to Brandes for a jazz concert – the first at the Köln Opera House.

At Jarrett's request, Vera has selected a Bosendorfer 290 Imperial concert grand piano for the performance. Due to a mix-up with the venue's piano on the day of the concert, Vera realizes that the only instrument available for the concert is a much smaller, old, out-of-tune, and poorly maintained Bosendorfer baby grand piano. The instrument is in such a dire state that even some of the keys are sticking, making it virtually unplayable. The piano is intended for rehearsals only, is in poor condition, and requires several hours of tuning and adjustment to make it playable.

The instrument is tinny and thin in the upper registers and weak in the bass register, and the pedals do not work properly.

Vera makes an attempt to procure another grand piano up to Jarrett's standards that can be delivered quickly. The piano tuner, who has meanwhile arrived to fix the baby grand, warned her that transporting a grand piano without the proper equipment at low temperatures in the middle of a rainstorm would irreparably damage the instrument. Vera is stuck with the small one.

It's pouring rain and Jarrett refuses to play. He leaves the opera house.

Vera is on the verge of tears. She goes out and finds Jarrett sitting in his car, waiting to be driven back to his hotel. She knocks on the window. Jarrett slowly turns and sees this young kid drenched by the rain.

Vera begs him. She pleads and tries to convince him that his musical talent can transcend any instrument, any circumstance. Jarrett takes a breath and turns to Vera and says, "Never forget. Only for you."

Once inside, Jarrett and his producer, Manfred Eicher, decide to record this concert as a cautionary tale. They want to document what happens when you don't give Jarrett the right piano.

Jarrett resolves to give it his all and decides to improvise his entire performance. Without any prepared compositions or setlist, he walks onto the stage and, against the backdrop of a skeptical audience, begins to play.

The result is pure magic.

Jarrett's raw talent channels a musical creativity that soars in the space. The acoustics of the venue add a unique resonance to each note, creating a mesmerizing atmosphere that captivates the audience.

After an hour and a half of listening to breathtaking melodies, harmonies, and rhythms, the crowd erupts into thunderous applause.

Despite the limitations of an imperfect piano and challenging circumstances, the music transcends everything, producing an extraordinary experience for the audience.

Jarrett doesn't just produce a decent performance. He produces what many people consider his best performance.

Thankfully for the rest of us, the performance is indeed recorded and is released as an album that quickly becomes a landmark in jazz music.

More than that, Keith Jarrett's album The Koln Concert is the best-selling jazz piano album of all time.

Let this story be an inspiration to embrace the creativity in all of us, regardless of circumstances.

You might just create something magical.

The Content Beast

21-Day Content Marketing Playbook

Week 1: Planning

Day 1: Identify Your Target Audience

Workbook Page 1: Define your target audience by filling out the following information:

- Age range:
- Gender:
- Education level completed:
- Income level:
- Occupation:
- Location:

Day 2: Set Marketing Goals

Workbook Page 2: Define your marketing goals by filling out the following information:

- Primary goal:
- Secondary goal:
- Metrics for measuring success:

Day 3: Conduct a Content Audit

Workbook Page 3: Conduct a content audit by filling out the following information:

- Content type:
- Title:
- Date published:
- Pageviews:
- Shares:
- Comments:

Day 4: Identify Content Gaps

Workbook Page 4: Identify content gaps by filling out the following information:
- Topic:
- Keywords:
- Format:
- Target audience:

Day 5: Create a Content Calendar

Workbook Page 5: Create a content calendar by filling out the following information:
- Date:
- Topic:
- Content type:
- Keywords:
- Author:
- Editor:
- Status:

Week 2: Content Creation

Day 6: Write A Blog Post

Workbook Page 6: Write a blog post by filling out the following information:
- Title:
- Topic:
- Keywords:
- Target audience:
- Outline:
- Draft:

Day 7: Design Social Media Graphics

Workbook Page 7: Design social media graphics by filling out the following information:
- Platform:
- Content type:
- Topic:
- Keywords:
- Design software used:
- Dimensions:
- Elements included:

Day 8: Record a Video

Workbook Page 8: Record a video by filling out the following information:
- Title:
- Topic:
- Keywords:
- Target audience:
- Outline:
- Script:
- Recording software used:

Day 9: Create a Lead Magnet

Workbook Page 9: Create a lead magnet by filling out the following information:
- Title:
- Topic:
- Keywords:
- Format:
- Target audience:
- Design software used:
- Distribution method:

Day 10: Write a Guest Post

Workbook Page 10: Write a guest post by filling out the following information:
- Title:
- Topic:
- Keywords:
- Target website:
- Outline:
- Draft:

Week 3: Promotion

Day 11: Share Content on Social Media

Workbook Page 11: Share content on social media by filling out the following information:
- Platform:
- Content type:
- Topic:
- Keywords:
- Hashtags used:
- Date and time posted:

Day 12: Outreach to Influencers

Workbook Page 12: Outreach to influencers by filling out the following information:
- Name of influencer:
- Platform:
- Reason for outreach:
- Pitch:
- Follow-up plan:

Day 13: Promote on LinkedIn

Workbook Page 13: Promote on LinkedIn by filling out the following information:
- Topic:
- Target audience:
- Groups to share in:
- Hashtags used:
- Date and time posted:

Day 14: Send Email Newsletter

Workbook Page 14: Send an email newsletter by filling out the following information:
- Subject line:
- Content type:
- Topics covered:
- Links included:
- List segment:
- Date and time sent:

Day 15: Repurpose Content

Workbook Page 15: Repurpose content by filling out the following information:
- Original content:
- Repurposed format:
- Target audience:
- Platform:
- Date and time posted:

Day 16: Host a Webinar

- Identify a topic that aligns with your content calendar and provides value to your target audience
- Host a webinar and promote it on your website, social media channels, and email list

Day 17: Conduct a Podcast Interview

- Reach out to relevant industry experts or influencers and invite them to be a guest on your podcast
- Promote the podcast on your website, social media channels, and email list

Day 18: Create Infographics

- Use data and information from your existing content to create visually appealing infographics
- Share the infographics on social media and in your email newsletter

Day 19: Participate in Online Communities

- Identify relevant online communities, such as LinkedIn groups or Facebook groups, where your target audience participates
- Share your content and engage with others in the community

Day 20: Host a Q&A Session

- Use your social media channels or website to host a Q&A session where you answer questions from your audience
- Encourage engagement by asking your audience to submit questions ahead of time

Day 21: Analyze Metrics and Adjust Strategy

- Use the metrics you set at the beginning of the 21-day plan to analyze the performance of your content marketing strategy
- Adjust your strategy based on what's working and what's not

Get your complete set of downloadable worksheets, bonuses, and companion tools by visiting thecontent-beast.co.

About the Author

Geoffrey Klein, aka Mr. Purple, is a TEDx and keynote speaker, an adjunct professor, and a visual content producer. He helps people and organizations communicate more effectively through the power of story.

Geoffrey's diverse professional experience includes working in the film industry to living in England, where he worked both in real estate and at a creative design agency.

Currently he serves as President & CEO of nine dots, a visual content company that helps businesses feed the Content Beast by producing video and animation content to connect with their audiences.

As a speaker, Geoffrey presents to audiences at conferences, associations, and corporate events.

Geoffrey has a bachelor's degree from Amherst College and a law degree from Temple University.

Geoffrey is a gadget and cufflinks enthusiast and Pez dispenser collector, and in his spare time he enjoys spending time with his wife and three children, whether it's baking, basketball, or board games.

Get in touch. Geoffrey@ninedotsmedia.com.